Original title:
Citrine Trails Beside the Faerie Clove

Copyright © 2025 Swan Charm
All rights reserved.

Author: Sebastian Sarapuu
ISBN HARDBACK: 978-1-80562-023-5
ISBN PAPERBACK: 978-1-80563-544-4

The Allure of Mystical Corners

In shadows deep where secrets dwell,
Whispers weave their timeless spell.
Ancient stones and twisted vines,
Invite the heart to wend the signs.

With every path, a story told,
Of dreams in silver, tales of gold.
Beneath the arch of twilight skies,
The allure of magic softly lies.

Illumination Among the Woodland Spirits

A glimmer glows in the forest heart,
Where life and light begin to part.
Among the trunks, the spirits sway,
Their laughter dances, night meets day.

Moonbeams filter through the leaves,
Crafting patterns that one believes.
This realm of wonder, wild and free,
Holds whispers of eternity.

Faerie Footprints in the Gilded Mist

In the golden haze of dew-kissed morn,
The faeries tread, their joy reborn.
With every step, a shimmer trails,
A hint of wonder in soft gales.

Luminous sparks 'neath ancient oaks,
A language sung in gentle strokes.
To find their path, one seeks with heart,
For magic weaves, and dreams depart.

Celestial Labyrinths in the Glimmering Veil

In twilight's glow, the stars align,
Creating paths where starlight shines.
A labyrinth of dreams awaits,
Each turn revealing hidden fates.

The nightingale's song calls us near,
To wander where the skies are clear.
Through glimmering veils, the heart may roam,
In celestial realms, we find our home.

Secrets Wrapped in Golden Leaves

In autumn's grasp, the trees confide,
Their golden leaves, a secret guide.
Each flutter down, a whispered plea,
To seek the truth in mystery.

As seasons change, so do our dreams,
Flowing like rivers, weaving streams.
In the heart of fall, let us believe,
In the magic wrapped in golden leaves.

Dappled Sunbeams Beneath the Enchanted Boughs

In dappled light where shadows play,
The boughs above, a green ballet.
With laughter found in nature's song,
We wander free where we belong.

Beneath the canopies, secrets bloom,
In fragrant earth, dispelling gloom.
The sunbeams dance on vibrant ground,
In enchanted woods, joy is found.

Dusk's Embrace in the Enchanted Sanctuary

In twilight's glow, the shadows dance,
Whispers echo, a fleeting chance.
Stars awaken, a gentle sigh,
In the sanctuary, we let time fly.

Soft petals fall, draped in night,
Moonlight weaves a tapestry bright.
Echoes of laughter, a sweet refrain,
In this refuge, we feel no pain.

Ancient stones hum, secrets unfold,
Tales of magic, both timid and bold.
As dreams entwine, in the dusky light,
Hearts beat gently, a shared delight.

The trees hold hands, in silent trust,
In their embrace, we find our must.
Drifting softly, through realms unknown,
In dusk's embrace, we find our home.

Time stands still, as night befalls,
In the enchanted, where wonder calls.
Forever lost, in the soft twilight,
Together we wander, through endless night.

Glimmers of Time in the Sylvan Enclave

Amidst the ferns, where sunlight gleams,
Glimmers of time weave through our dreams.
Whispers of ages, in softest breeze,
Nature's secrets rest with ease.

With each step, the forest sighs,
Beneath the canopies, where magic lies.
In the glades, where shadows play,
Moments linger, then drift away.

Elfin melodies drift through the air,
Chasing the echoes, without a care.
The laughter of sprites, a cherished sound,
In this enclave, true peace is found.

Time dances slow, in the sylvan light,
Bathed in warmth, we hold on tight.
The heart blooms bright, in soft refrain,
In this sanctuary, we feel no pain.

As dusk descends, the stars emerge,
Illuminating paths, where feelings surge.
Together we wander, hand in hand,
Glimmers of time, in this enchanted land.

Silent Murmurs in the Glistening Clove

In the heart of the wood, shadows entwine,
Silent murmurs, a gentle sign.
Where leaves shimmer, like whispers soft,
In the clove's embrace, our spirits loft.

Moonbeams fall on a silken leaf,
Glistening bright, relieving grief.
Each sigh of the trees, a tale they'd tell,
Of longing, of love, in this hidden dell.

So closely held, the night reveals,
Wonders untouched, our heart it steals.
In every corner, a secret lies,
Beneath the stars, where silence flies.

A soft rustle, where dreams take flight,
In the glistening clove, all feels right.
As shadows blend, and stars ignite,
We dance in whispers, till morning light.

The world fades out, as magic winds,
Through glimmering paths, our hearts begins.
In stillness we find, the timeless glow,
Silent murmurs, where we must go.

Twilit Delights Amongst Ancient Trees

Amid ancient trunks, where shadows wane,
Twilit delights scatter like rain.
In hushed tones, the stories unfold,
Of magic spun, in threads of gold.

Moonlit beams touch the forest floor,
Inviting dreams to dance and soar.
With each step, in sweet harmony,
Amongst the trees, we find our glee.

Echoes of laughter, carried by the breeze,
In this refuge, a life to seize.
Leaves whisper secrets, from days of yore,
In their presence, we long for more.

Graced by night, where wishes bloom,
In twilit embrace, we chase the gloom.
The past and the present, intertwined,
In this magic, our souls aligned.

As stars unveil their midnight glow,
Amongst ancient trees, we start to know.
In every heart, the joy's release,
Twilit delights, our sweet solace.

Beneath the Bark of Amber Stories

In the heart of the woods, a tale begins,
Where secrets are kept, by the squirrel's spins.
The amber glow wraps each whispery night,
With stories unfolding in soft, golden light.

Old trees hold their breath, in the shimmering haze,
As echoes of laughter drift through the maze.
With every rustle, a new mystery wakes,
Beneath the bark, where the magic takes.

Moss-clad roots gather, like dreams intertwined,
While shadows dance lightly, in forms undefined.
An owl silently watches with wise, knowing eyes,
As the moon hums a tune through the starry skies.

A fox with a flicker darts quick through the ferns,
In each rustling whisper, a hidden world turns.
Beneath the amber, where wonders reside,
Lies a tapestry woven with nature as guide.

As twilight embroiders the canvas of night,
The stories awaken, glowing so bright.
Each creature, it seems, plays a part in the tale,
Beneath the bark, where the whispers won't pale.

The Soft Glow of Forest Whimsy

In a glen where the giggles of fairies swirl,
Dewdrops like diamonds dance in a twirl.
The soft glow of whimsy enchants all who tread,
With laughter and joy weaving pathways ahead.

Tall trees weave their branches, a canopy grand,
Where dreams take to flight on the wispiest sand.
Toadstools stand guard, bright colors adorned,
In the heart of the forest, a magic is born.

The brook sings a tune, with a glimmer and glee,
As whispers of wishes float soft through the trees.
With each step, a flutter, a new charm revealed,
In the soft glow of forest, the world is healed.

Sunbeams peek through, like a gentle embrace,
Capturing moments with delicate grace.
Each corner a canvas, new stories ignite,
In the soft glow of whims, all the world feels right.

As the day melts away, in hues warm and bright,
The whispers of twilight dance into the night.
With stars gathered closely, the forest will gleam,
In the heart of the whimsy, we find our sweet dreams.

Whispers of Light Through the Enchanted Pastures

In the softest of meadows where magic resides,
Whispers of light paint the earth as it glides.
Each blade of tall grass sways tender and free,
As daylight unfolds, a sweet melody.

Gentle flutters of wings cross the sunbeams bright,
While petals unfurl, basking warmly in light.
The enchantment awakens, a spell in the air,
Guiding hearts softly through lands rich and rare.

A brook babbles secrets with sparkling delight,
Leading dreams onward, through day into night.
With every soft sigh, a new wish is spun,
In the enchanted pastures, where wanderers run.

As sun kisses earth with its warm, golden touch,
Nature hums softly, oh, how we love such!
In the whispers of light, through the lush emerald,
A story unfolds, full of wonder and gold.

With twilight approaching, hues blend and collide,
Magic lingers sweetly, where shadows reside.
In whispers of light, memories twine and dance,
In enchanted pastures, we lose ourselves, perchance.

Faerie Whispers Beneath the Crescent Glow

In twilight's dance, where faeries play,
They twirl and spin 'neath moonlit sway.
With laughter sweet, and gleaming eyes,
They weave their dreams 'neath starlit skies.

Soft whispers float on evening's air,
Tales of old, both wondrous and rare.
In shadows cast by silver beams,
They share their hopes and hidden dreams.

Each flitting spark, a story told,
Of lost enchantments, brave and bold.
Beyond the trees, where magic stirs,
The heart awakens, as vision blurs.

Dance, little faeries, with hearts so light,
Beneath the crescent's soft, glowing light.
For in your world of laughter and grace,
We find our joy, our sacred place.

Light and Shadow in the Faerie Grove

In the faerie grove, where shadows merge,
Light and dark in a gentle surge.
A flicker here, a rustle there,
Secrets pulse in the fragrant air.

Twilight whispers, secrets concealed,
In the heart of woods, magic revealed.
Beams of gold through leaves cascade,
Illuminating dreams that never fade.

Glimmers of hope in whispers low,
Guide the way where wonders grow.
With every step, a tale unfolds,
In the borderless realm where love beholds.

Embrace the night, let your heart roam,
In the faerie grove, you find your home.
A symphony of shadows and light,
Casts a spell that feels just right.

Journeys through the Whispering Enigma

Through tangled paths and secret ways,
We journey forth, through misty haze.
Each turn a mystery yet untold,
A whispering enigma waiting bold.

Tall trees stand guard, their branches sway,
Guiding lost souls who find their way.
With every step, a world unfolds,
In hidden realms where destiny holds.

The murmurs of ages past breathe near,
Echoing memories we hold dear.
A heart beats strong, a voice so clear,
Leading us onward through joy and fear.

With every choice, a path we weave,
In dreams of magic, we believe.
Through twilight's veil, our spirits soar,
Journey onward, to forevermore.

Golden Fables of the Twilight Realm

In the twilight realm where tales are spun,
Golden fables shine, one by one.
With each heartbeat, a legend grows,
In the sacred light, where wonder glows.

Whispers of love in the gentle breeze,
Dance through the branches of ancient trees.
Stories linger in the evening air,
Crafting the magic we all can share.

Fabled creatures with hearts of gold,
Teach us the wisdom that never grows old.
In twilight's embrace, beneath starlit skies,
We find our courage, and learn to rise.

Golden dreams of a world unseen,
Awaken our hearts, like sunlight gleam.
For in every story, a truth holds fast—
The love we nurture forever lasts.

Golden Pathways Through Enchanted Woods

Through golden pathways, soft and bright,
The whispering woods invite the light.
With every step, the magic stirs,
Amongst the trees, the mystery purrs.

Sunbeams dance on emerald leaves,
In this realm, the heart believes.
Secrets hid in shadows deep,
Are woven dreams the woods will keep.

With laughter of the gentle breeze,
And rustling tales from ancient trees,
A journey where the wild things roam,
In nature's heart, we find our home.

Beneath the arch of tangled vines,
Where every glance the heart entwines,
The golden light, it warmly calls,
To those who heed the forest's thralls.

So take a breath, let worries cease,
In golden pathways, find your peace.
Among the leaves, let spirits soar,
In enchanted woods, forevermore.

Whispers of Light Beneath the Canopy

In twilight hues, the whispers grow,
Beneath the canopy, mysteries flow.
A gentle murmur, a soft embrace,
Where shadows dance in a hidden place.

The light it weaves through branches high,
Kissing the soil, where secrets lie.
With every rustle and sighing breeze,
Nature's language, it aims to please.

From dappled paths to shimmering streams,
Awake the world of starlit dreams.
The songs of dusk begin to play,
On whispered winds that softly sway.

In veins of green, the heartbeats thrived,
With every pulse, the world alive.
A tapestry of life unfurls,
With stories told in ethereal swirls.

So linger here, let worries fall,
Beneath the canopy, hear the call.
In whispers of light, let souls align,
With nature's wonder, pure and divine.

Secrets of the Sunlit Glade

In the sunlit glade, where dreams take flight,
Secrets shimmer in the golden light.
Beneath the boughs, the spirits play,
Spinning tales in a gentle sway.

Wildflowers bloom like colorful gems,
Each petal sings, each leaf condemns.
The echoes of laughter fill the air,
In this sacred space, we find our care.

The warmth of sun on soft, cool ground,
Where whispered wishes can be found.
A portal to magic when day meets night,
The glade's secrets bask in delight.

In gentle breezes, old tales are told,
Of brave souls and treasures of gold.
The gentle hum of life revealed,
Awaits the heart that's truly healed.

So come and wander, let spirit roam,
In the sunlit glade, we find our home.
With secrets woven in nature's thread,
In its embrace, we're gently led.

Dappled Dreams in Sylvan Hues

In dappled dreams where shadows lie,
The sylvan hues catch the wandering eye.
Each moment golden, time feels vast,
In a tranquil world, we drift and bask.

With softly spoken tales of old,
Whispers of magic, silent and bold.
Where the sunlight threads through byzantine leaves,
And nature's charm the spirit weaves.

A symphony of rustles in the underbrush,
The world awakens in a gentle hush.
Through tangled paths, adventure calls,
In dappled dreams, the heart enthralls.

So close your eyes, let visions bloom,
In every shade, let your heart resume.
With every breath a story grows,
In sylvan hues, the magic flows.

So wander here, let worries slide,
In nature's cradle, hearts abide.
With dappled dreams that softly fuse,
Embrace the magic, know it's yours to choose.

Golden Pathways through Enchanted Woods

Through winding trails of emerald hue,
Golden leaves dance, kissed by dew.
Whispers of magic fill the air,
Underneath the branches, secrets share.

Roots entwined in stories old,
Sunlight catches glimmers gold.
Steps lead forth, where dreams may start,
In the woods, a wanderer's heart.

Mossy carpets beneath their feet,
Nature's rhythm, a gentle beat.
Fairy laughter, soft as silk,
Sipping from the cup of milk.

Petals flutter, colors bright,
Guiding spirits in the night.
Among the trees, the magic swells,
As every leaf, a story tells.

Journey bound to realms concealed,
In each step, new wonders revealed.
The golden pathways gently wind,
Through enchanted woods, truths unwind.

Mystical Glimmers in Twilight Glades

In twilight's grasp, soft shadows fall,
A symphony of night's sweet call.
Glimmers twinkle in fading light,
As fireflies dance, a wondrous sight.

Whispers echo through the trees,
Carried softly on the breeze.
The glades awake, a hidden charm,
Where nature weaves her gentle calm.

Rippling streams weave tales of old,
Carrying dreams in waters bold.
Moss-clad stones, a resting place,
Embraced by shadows, a warm embrace.

A silver moon, a watchful eye,
Sees secrets pass as hours fly.
Each glimmer speaks of ancient lore,
In twilight glades, forevermore.

Dancing shadows, soft and fleet,
Chant a hymn, an ancient beat.
Where hearts arise to meet the night,
In mystical glimmers, pure delight.

Whispering Shadows of the Amber Grove

In amber groves, the shadows play,
Cascading light at end of day.
Whispers linger in the hush,
Where time slows down in gentle rush.

Beneath the boughs, where secrets grow,
Murmurs of the past still flow.
Every rustle and every sigh,
Weaves the fabric of the sky.

Starlit paths on dusky ground,
With veils of mist, enchantment found.
In every breath, the earth unfolds,
Tales of warmth, as daylight folds.

Crimson leaves in soft embrace,
Join the dance of twilight's grace.
A symphony of night, so grand,
In amber groves, take a stand.

Listen close to the night's sweet tune,
A lullaby beneath the moon.
Where shadows whisper, secrets deep,
In amber groves, find dreams to keep.

Sunlit Echoes of the Forgotten Glade

In forgotten glades where sunbeams play,
Echoes linger, fading away.
Whispers of laughter, soft and clear,
Call to the heart, drawing near.

Where flowers bloom in colors bright,
Bringing warmth to morning light.
Petals flutter like gentle sighs,
As nature sings of whispered ties.

Tangled vines and ancient trees,
Guard the stories carried on the breeze.
A tapestry of sunlit dreams,
In forgotten glades, life redeems.

Time stands still in this sacred place,
Paved in memories, woven grace.
Where every echo dares to gleam,
In golden rays, we dare to dream.

Gather the moments, let them unfold,
In the beauty of life, rich and bold.
Sunlit echoes renew each soul,
In the forgotten glade, we are whole.

The Radiance of Lost Grove Secrets

In a grove where shadows dance,
Ancient whispers weave romance.
Twinkling lights like fireflies,
Guard the secrets, old and wise.

Softly rustling leaves above,
Echo tales of forgotten love.
Mossy stones and gnarled roots,
Hold the mystique of hidden truths.

Into the depths, a lantern glows,
Illuminating all that knows.
Footsteps light on emerald trails,
Echoing the heart's soft wails.

Caught between the worlds of night,
Magic shimmers, pure delight.
Each breath a song, a gentle call,
In the grove, we find it all.

Beneath the stars, old spirits sigh,
A promise made, a binding tie.
In hushed tones, the secrets grow,
In the grove, where dreams bestow.

Amber Dreams in the Whispering Vale

In the vale where shadows play,
Amber dreams take flight and sway.
Whispers float on the evening air,
Tales of magic everywhere.

Golden hues and twilight's grace,
Cradle every fleeting place.
Flowers bloom and softly sigh,
Beneath the watchful, starlit sky.

Rustling grasses greet the night,
Dancing softly, pure delight.
Every breeze, a gentle kiss,
A song of longing, woven bliss.

Winding paths where secrets blend,
Echoes of the past ascend.
A land where every heart may roam,
In the vale, we find our home.

With every dream, the stars align,
In amber light, the fates combine.
Together we weave hopes anew,
In the vale, where magic's true.

Sylvan Journeys through Glistening Ferns

Through glistening ferns, the path awaits,
Nature's breath, where time abates.
Footsteps whisper on the ground,
In this silence, truth is found.

Winding trails through emerald grace,
Mark the heart's most sacred place.
Sunbeams dance on dewy fronds,
Opening portals to our bonds.

Mossy seats beneath the trees,
Cradle dreams upon the breeze.
Each leaf murmurs untold lore,
With a promise of something more.

Swaying softly in the glade,
Life unfolds, unafraid.
Lost in wonder, wild and free,
In sylvan realms, we're meant to be.

As twilight falls, the stars appear,
Guiding all who venture near.
With each heartbeat, nature blends,
In the ferns, the journey bends.

When Sunlight Meets the Mystical Realm

When sunlight meets the mystical realm,
Ethereal wonders take the helm.
Golden rays through branches filter,
A dance of light, a heart's soft spilter.

In this space where dreams reside,
Magic breathes, the world's a guide.
Each ray a thread of cosmic fate,
Woven close, we resonate.

Boundless whispers in the air,
Enchant the soul, bring peace and care.
Nature's palette glows and shines,
Through every moment, love entwines.

Time dissolves in the sacred light,
Holding shadows, chasing night.
In harmony, the spirits call,
When sunlight gleams, we find our all.

So, step within this realm of dreams,
Where nothing is quite as it seems.
In every glow, a tale unfolds,
When sunlight speaks, the heart beholds.

Starlit Whispers Through the Golden Glimmer

In the realm where shadows dance,
Stars whisper secrets, lost in trance.
Golden glimmers paint the night,
Crafting dreams in silver light.

Through enchanted woods, the moon shall tread,
Guiding hearts where all is said.
Beneath the vast and twinkling skies,
Magic stirs, and wonder flies.

In gardens where the fireflies roam,
Ethereal whispers call us home.
A tapestry of fate unfolds,
As timeless lore in silence holds.

Every sigh, a story shared,
In twilight's grasp, the soul laid bare.
With each breath, the world delights,
In starlit whispers, love ignites.

So take my hand, and walk with me,
Through golden glimmers, wild and free.
Where every star holds dreams of yore,
We'll find the magic evermore.

Honeyed Melodies on Whispering Winds

Softly sings the breeze above,
Carrying tales of loss and love.
Honeyed scents and laughter blend,
As nature's symphony ascends.

Rustling leaves in twilight glow,
Echo secrets only we know.
Melodies on gentle streams,
Flow through the fabric of our dreams.

With every note, the heart does race,
In this enchanted, sacred space.
Through towering oaks and fields of gold,
Wonderous stories yearn to be told.

The sun dips low, its warmth we chase,
Dancing shadows leave a trace.
As dusk enfolds the vibrant day,
The honeyed melodies gently sway.

So let your spirit freely glide,
On whispering winds, let fears subside.
For in each tune, the world aligns,
In harmony, our heart entwines.

Glints of Elegance in Nature's Embrace

Dew-kissed petals glisten bright,
Embraced by morning's tender light.
Nature's gown, a rich display,
In glorious hues of green and gray.

Streams weave whispers, soft and sweet,
Carving paths where shadows meet.
Birdsongs ripple through the air,
A delicate dance both pure and rare.

On velvet hills where wildflowers sigh,
Elegance breathes beneath the sky.
Every rustle, every sigh,
Crafts a tale of days gone by.

The sun's warm glow on our skin,
Promising joy—life can begin.
In nature's embrace, we find our peace,
As all our worries gently cease.

So close your eyes, let worries fade,
In glints of elegance, unafraid.
For in this sanctuary divine,
We bloom like flowers, intertwine.

The Soft Sparkle of Forgotten Dreams

In quiet corners of the mind,
Forgotten dreams, lost yet kind.
Whispers linger on the breeze,
Softly stirring memories with ease.

Once they sparkled, bright and bold,
Now softly draped in stories told.
Like stardust scattered through the haze,
They shimmer faint in twilight's gaze.

Each flicker, a promise held tight,
Cradled softly in the night.
Echoes of laughter, soft and clear,
Drawing closer, holding dear.

Let us wander through these trails,
Where time unfurls, where magic sails.
In the quiet, we'll reminisce,
For forgotten dreams can't be amiss.

So breathe them in, these flickers light,
A gentle guide through the velvet night.
For in their glow, we find our way,
To spark anew, to dream and play.

Enchantment's Embrace in Sylvan Retreat

In shadows deep where whispers sigh,
The trees entwine beneath the sky.
With leaves that dance in moonlit beams,
A realm awash in silvery dreams.

The brook hums songs of ages past,
While time itself slips by so fast.
Each step unveils a mystic trail,
Where echoes of the forest wail.

An owl takes flight on silent wings,
In twilight's hush, the heart still sings.
All creatures pause in nature's thrall,
As night descends to clasp us all.

In enchanted glades, the fae do play,
With laughter bright that steals away.
Their magic swirls in vibrant hues,
A hidden world to dream and choose.

So linger here in twilight's grace,
Find solace in this sacred space.
For in each heart, the wild does dwell,
In whispered spells, all secrets tell.

Woven Dreams in the Illuminated Wilds

Beneath the stars where starlight weaves,
A tapestry of hopes and leaves.
The night unfolds with secrets spun,
In glades where wild and wonder run.

The brook that babbles, soft and low,
Carries whispers from long ago.
Each echo dances on the breeze,
Enfolding hearts with gentle ease.

In silver glow, the shadows play,
As fireflies light the dusky way.
With every flicker, dreams take flight,
In woodland's embrace, through the night.

The hidden paths with stories roam,
Invite the weary heart back home.
For in these woods of lore and light,
Lives magic bright, a pure delight.

So let your spirit freely soar,
Discover realms forevermore.
With woven dreams, the wild awaits,
Unlock the doors to mystic gates.

Mysterious Glows of the Nature's Heart

In secret glens where shadows blend,
The heart of nature does extend.
With glowing orbs and gentle charms,
It wraps all souls in quiet arms.

The moonlight filters through thick trees,
A silver kiss upon the breeze.
While nature's pulse, both strong and true,
Reveals its wonders, old and new.

Soft rustlings hint at what may be,
A world awake, yet wild and free.
Each glow that flares ignites the night,
A mystery cloaked in mystic light.

For here within this sacred space,
All beings find a soft embrace.
So linger long, let silence speak,
In glimmers bright, find what you seek.

The whispers call from leafy bows,
Join in the dance where magic glows.
In nature's heart, where dreams unfurl,
Discover depths of a hidden world.

Serendipity in the Amber-tinted Meadow

In fields where sunlight gently pours,
The golden grain, a dream restores.
With every breeze, a song is sung,
A symphony of earth well-spun.

The daisies sway, the lilies nod,
In nature's realm, all paths applaud.
Each vibrant hue, a brush of fate,
In meadows wide, love's dance awaits.

Amidst the blooms, serendipity calls,
With laughter bright that never falls.
The buzz of bees, a joyful sound,
In this sweet sanctuary found.

The rustling grass, a whispered plea,
Invites the heart to wander free.
For in each step, the world aligns,
A tapestry where wonder shines.

So pause a while, take in the view,
With every glance, the heart renews.
In amber meadows, dreams will swell,
Serendipity casts its spell.

Shimmering Secrets Among Wildflowers

In gardens wide where colors dance,
Bewitched by blooms in sunlit trance.
With whispers soft the petals sway,
They guard the secrets of the day.

A honeyed scent upon the breeze,
Beneath the watch of ancient trees.
The flutter of a faerie's wing,
Hints of the magic spring will bring.

A sunlight patch on emerald ground,
In every flower, dreams abound.
Hidden voices in the air,
Sharing tales of love and care.

Where wild and free the critters roam,
Each blossom calls the heart to home.
Life's tapestry in vibrant hues,
Taught by nature's timeless views.

As dusk descends on petals bright,
The stars emerge, soft glimmers light.
In quiet realms where secrets lie,
The wildflowers bloom, and spirits fly.

Radiant Footsteps in the Eldertree Realm

In Eldertree where shadows play,
The ancient roots hold tales of day.
With every step on mossy ground,
The echoes of the past resound.

A dance of light through leaves so green,
Unfolds the beauty, yet unseen.
The whispers of the ancients call,
In harmony, we heed their thrall.

With branches swaying in the air,
The secrets woven everywhere.
The rustling leaves, a gentle song,
Guide us where we all belong.

The fireflies twinkle, softly glow,
Illuminating paths we know.
Each footprint etched in fragile night,
A memory held, forever bright.

In Eldertree, where wonder dwells,
The heart entwined with ancient spells.
A realm where dreams and echoes blend,
Where every journey finds its end.

Autumn's Touch on the Enchanted Grove

In enchanted groves where time does rest,
Autumn's touch, a painter blessed.
With golden leaves that crisp and curl,
A tapestry begins to unfurl.

The whispers of the wind do sigh,
As branches bow and seasons fly.
Beneath the oaks, the secrets lie,
Of passing mornings, sweet goodbye.

A harvest moon that lights the way,
Guides wanderers through twilight's play.
Each step a story softly told,
In vibrant hues of red and gold.

With gentle grace the shadows weave,
Offering gifts of time to believe.
A melody of rustling leaves,
That lingers long, as daylight leaves.

Together we embrace the chill,
In heart's warm glow, we find our will.
For autumn dances in the air,
A season filled with love and care.

Gilded Wanderings Through Mystical Ferns

In forests deep, where secrets weave,
The ferns unfold, and hearts believe.
With emerald fronds that catch the light,
A world awakens in soft night.

Each shadowed path invites the soul,
To dance within the ancient whole.
With every step, the magic calls,
As moonlit beams through canopy falls.

The whispers of the woodland fair,
Entwine with dreams that linger there.
In gilded shades of green's embrace,
We find our magic, take our place.

A symphony of rustling sounds,
Among the ferns, where joy surrounds.
Captured moments, fleeting, bright,
In every glimpse, a spark of light.

With hearts aglow, the wanderers roam,
In mystical realms, we find our home.
Nature's song in every turn,
For in the ferns, our spirits yearn.

Enchanted Paths of Golden Dust

Upon the trail where whispers play,
Golden dust in sunlight's sway,
Each step a secret, softly spun,
In laughter's echo, dreams begun.

Through ancient woods where shadows dance,
Magic lingers, sweet romance,
Beneath the boughs, the fairies weave,
A tapestry of night to believe.

The murmurs of the brook nearby,
Carry tales that never die,
As twilight falls, the fireflies rise,
A fleeting beauty never lies.

With every breath, the silence hums,
A promise of what soon becomes,
A heart alight with hope and grace,
In every nook, a warm embrace.

So tread with care on paths of light,
For magic dwells in every sight,
In golden dust, our spirits soar,
Embracing what we can't ignore.

The Glow of Missed Moments in Fairyland

In twilight's hue, the world retold,
Whispers dance in warmth so bold,
The glow of moments passed us by,
Like fireflies caught in a sigh.

Among the glades where time stands still,
Memories blossom in e'er green hill,
Each twinkle hints of what could be,
In Fairyland's soft reverie.

Once spoken words now float like leaves,
Carried on a breeze that grieves,
Yet in their silence, lessons glow,
A chance to learn, to seek, to grow.

With every rustle, stories weave,
A patchwork quilt of all we believe,
In the hush, a bittersweet charm,
That echoes softly to disarm.

So linger here, o'er paths of night,
With every shadow, love's pure light,
For in this realm where dreams align,
The glow of missed moments will always shine.

Boughs Weaving Tales of Golden Light

Underneath the sprawling trees,
Boughs entwined in gentle ease,
They whisper soft, old tales anew,
Of joy and sorrow, me and you.

In their embrace, the shadows play,
Casting dreams that drift away,
Beneath the canopy so wide,
A refuge where our hopes can bide.

With every rustling leaf, we hear,
The laughter of those once held dear,
The golden threads of time connect,
In boughs that weave and so reflect.

Stories linger in the air,
Of wanderlust, of love laid bare,
For every swirl of autumn's breath,
Tells of life and even death.

So let us walk where boughs meet sky,
With openness and spirits high,
For every tale in golden light,
Gives wings to dreams that soar in flight.

Liquid Gold in the Heart of the Trees

In secret glades where shadows gleam,
A river flows like whispered dream,
Liquid gold through roots and stone,
A magic crafted, ever grown.

The heart of trees, a silent beat,
Echoing softly, oh so sweet,
Each drop a story, rich and deep,
In nature's hands, the secrets keep.

With every swirl, the thoughts entwine,
Binding earth and spirit's line,
In liquid gold, the truth is found,
As laughter mingles with the ground.

So bend your ear and drink it in,
The rustling trees, the tales begin,
With every sip, a memory stirs,
In harmony with nature's blurs.

Embrace the magic, feel the flow,
In the heart of trees where wonders grow,
For in this space, both wild and free,
Lives the purest essence of thee.

The Luminescent Journey of Woodland Spirits

In twilight's grasp, where shadows play,
The spirits gather, soft and gay.
With whispered winds, their laughter swells,
They dance beneath the ancient bells.

Through silver streams and leafy glades,
They glide on dreams, in secret shades.
Illuminated by the stars' delight,
Their glowing forms take flight at night.

Each step they take, the flowers sigh,
As moonlit paths begin to fly.
With every shimmer, hopes arise,
In harmony with night's disguise.

A journey spun of whispers keen,
In every shadow, unseen sheen.
Together bound by nature's art,
Their glowing tales, a world apart.

In the heart where magic sleeps,
The woodland's secret gently creeps.
With every flicker, truth is found,
A cosmic dance in twilight's sound.

Honeyed Echoes in the Fairy Hollow

In the hollow where echoes play,
Fairy whispers blend with the day.
A scent of nectar fills the air,
As hazy dreams enchant the fair.

From dewdrop cups, the sunlight spills,
As shimmering light the forest thrills.
With every buzz and gentle hum,
The sweetness sings, the fairies come.

Beneath the boughs where secrets sigh,
The trailing vines in laughter lie.
They weave a song, so soft, so sweet,
A honeyed echo at our feet.

With sparkling eyes and joyful hearts,
The forest hums, in life it starts.
Each fluttered wing brings tales anew,
In this enchanted panorama's view.

As twilight cloaks the vibrant scene,
Fairy laughter glints like a dream.
In the hollow, magic blooms,
Where honeyed echoes chase the glooms.

Glimmers of Amber on Moss-Kissed Stones

Upon the stones, moss-kissed and bright,
Glimmers of amber dance in light.
Each droplet caught in sunlit beams,
A testament to nature's dreams.

The forest floor, a tapestry,
Of greens and golds, a sight to see.
Where every shimmer tells a tale,
Of woodland whispers on the trail.

Between the roots, where silence sways,
The amber's glow softly plays.
A fleeting moment, pure and sweet,
As twilight's cloak begins to greet.

With gentle sighs, the branches sway,
As shadows dance and drift away.
In every nook, a secret lies,
As amber glimmers dimmed in sighs.

The world awakens, life anew,
With every hue beneath the dew.
These moss-kissed stones, a sacred place,
Where time is lost in nature's grace.

The Brightness Between Twinkling Leaves

In dappled light, the leaves embrace,
A hidden warmth, a gentle space.
Where sunbeams spill and shadows weave,
A brilliance found in twilight's cleave.

Through verdant paths, the whispers twine,
As twinkling stars in daylight shine.
In rustling songs, their secrets flow,
Creating dreams where rhythms glow.

The fluttering wings of passing sprites,
Bathe in the glow of fading lights.
Each leaf a story, bright and bold,
Of adventures shared, and tales retold.

Amidst the trees where moments blend,
The brightness grows and will not end.
With every rustle, hearts entwine,
In nature's magic, pure, divine.

So linger here, in this embrace,
Where bright illusions find their place.
Among the leaves, let spirits weave,
In the bright magic twilight leaves.

Dances of Light in Shadowed Corners

In corners where shadows creep,
The whispers of light gently sweep.
Soft beams twirl like a silken thread,
In the dance of dreams, where hope is fed.

Glimmers of joy in the darkest night,
Filling the air with a warm, soft light.
Each flicker a story, each spark a song,
In the heart of the stillness, where shadows belong.

Awaking the magic that lies in the gloom,
The dance of the light begins to bloom.
With every swirl, a tale unfolds,
Of hidden wishes and secrets untold.

Laughter cascades like a misty veil,
As forgotten dreams begin to sail.
Through the veil of night, they elegantly glide,
Dancing amidst the shadows, side by side.

Encounters along the Magical Threshold

At the edge of the world, where magic is spun,
Adventures await, endlessly begun.
Each doorway a whisper, a call to explore,
With secrets and wonders forever in store.

Meet me at twilight, where dreams do collide,
In the realms of enchantment, where whispers reside.
The threshold beckons with mysteries rare,
An invitation to journey, if only we dare.

Old stones breathe stories of ages long past,
While shimmering orbs in the twilight cast.
They flicker with hope, they shimmer with grace,
Inviting all dreamers to join in the chase.

Each step is a promise, each turn a delight,
In the heart of the magic, where day meets the night.
With laughter and wonder, our spirits take flight,
Together we'll venture, embracing the light.

Twilight Enchantment Among the Autumn Leaves

When daylight surrenders to dusk's sweet embrace,
The world is adorned in a glittering lace.
Golden and crimson, the leaves gently sway,
In the symphony whispered by autumn's ballet.

Beneath the old oak, where shadows now grow,
Stories unfold in the soft evening glow.
Each rustle a secret, each flutter a kiss,
In the twilight enchantment, we find our bliss.

The air is a potion, rich with delight,
Transporting us softly to realms of pure light.
With friends gathered near, we share our old tales,
As laughter and magic dance through the gales.

The stars peek above, as we cherish the night,
Amongst all the colors, our hearts take flight.
In the spell of the autumn, where dreams are spun,
We bask in the magic, till morning's begun.

The Enigma of Glittering Petals

In a garden of wonder, where whispers reside,
The petals are secrets that dreams cannot hide.
They shimmer in moonlight, a luminous dance,
A tapestry woven by fate and chance.

Each hue tells a story, each bloom sings a song,
In the depths of the night, where the heart feels belonging.

A mystery unfolds with each gentle sigh,
Beneath the starlit canvas that stretches so high.

The breeze carries laughter, as petals take flight,
A wafting reminder of joy and delight.
Embroidered with magic, their beauty is rare,
A chorus of colors floats softly in air.

A moment of stillness, where dreams find their way,
In the enigma of petals, we long to stay.
For hidden among blooms, we discover our part,
Embraced by the magic that dances the heart.

Luminous Adventures in the Hidden Glen

In a glen where whispers dwell,
The light dances, casting a spell.
Beneath the boughs of ancient trees,
Secrets float on the gentle breeze.

Crickets hum in symphony,
As fireflies twirl and softly flee.
Each step taken, magic ignites,
Drawing forth the starry nights.

A brook gurgles with tales untold,
Of hopes and dreams in whispers bold.
Where dew-kissed petals freely sway,
Every moment, a wondrous ballet.

The shadows play, and colors blend,
In this place, where wonders mend.
With every heartbeat, worlds collide,
Together, our spirits glide.

In the hidden glen, dreams take flight,
Adventures bloom in twilight's light.
So wander here with heart ablaze,
And rival the sun's warm rays.

The Faerie's Dream in Amber Light

In amber light where faeries weave,
A tapestry of dreams to believe.
Softly glowing, their laughter rings,
As night unfurls its silver wings.

A moonlit path of shimmering dust,
Leads us through the dreams we trust.
With wings aglow like stars that gleam,
They guide us gently through the dream.

Whispers of magic in the air,
The faerie's song, a jeweled prayer.
Each note a wish, each pause a sigh,
Connecting earth with the boundless sky.

Through twilight's hue, we dance and twirl,
In that enchanted, swirling whirl.
With spirits lifted, fears take flight,
In this faerie dream of amber light.

So close your eyes and find the key,
To unlock a world wild and free.
In dreams we leap, and in dreams we soar,
The faerie's realm forevermore.

Glimmers off the Faerie's Kingdom

Glimmers dance like stardust bright,
Off the faerie's kingdom in moonlight.
A realm where laughter fills the air,
And every heart has joys to share.

Silver streams like ribbons flow,
Beneath the boughs where wildflowers grow.
In the twilight, colors collide,
As dreams and wishes gently guide.

With each glimmer, magic unfolds,
Stories of adventure, brave and bold.
A tapestry woven with love and care,
In the faerie's kingdom, free of despair.

The stars cascade like gentle rain,
A celestial dance, our hearts' domain.
With every twinkle, hope expands,
In this wondrous land where kindness stands.

So follow the glimmers, let them show,
The hidden paths where joy can grow.
In the faerie's dance, we find our way,
Glowing brightly at the end of the day.

Serene Walks Through Amber Hues

In the heart of twilight's gentle sigh,
Serene walks where amber skies lie.
Each step whispers softly of peace,
As the rush of day begins to cease.

A carpet of leaves in colors aglow,
Guides our journey as breezes blow.
With every heartbeat, tranquility sings,
In the warmth of the love that nature brings.

The horizon blushes in golden light,
As dreams awaken and hearts take flight.
We wander through hues of soft embrace,
Finding solace in this sacred space.

Every rustle, a secret untold,
In the stillness, let our stories unfold.
With every moment, joy reappears,
In these serene walks through amber years.

So linger a while in this tranquil zone,
Where the whispers of nature feel like home.
With eyes that shine and spirits bright,
We merge into the magic of the night.

Of Magic and Light on Hidden Routes

In forest deep where secrets dwell,
A whispering breeze begins to tell.
Paths adorned with glimmers bright,
Of magic's grace and ancient light.

The roots entwined, a tale unfolds,
Of heroes great and quests of old.
With every step, the shadows play,
A dance of night, a beckoning day.

Through glen and grove, the echoes sing,
Of fabled beasts and wondrous things.
The air ignites with stories bold,
Where dreams ignite and hearts behold.

The lantern's glow, a guiding spark,
In the hidden trails, we leave our mark.
With laughter soaring, spirits high,
Together we weave, just you and I.

So journey forth, beneath the skies,
In every corner, magic lies.
With hands entwined, let's chase the night,
On hidden routes of magic and light.

Sunbeams Dancing with the Woodland Fae

In morning's glow, the sunbeams weave,
A tapestry of light to believe.
Amongst the trees, the fae take flight,
In shimmering dance, a wondrous sight.

Their laughter rings like chimes of gold,
As stories of old are gently told.
The petals sway, the leaves entwine,
In nature's realm, all hearts align.

With every twirl, the flowers bloom,
Casting away the shadow's gloom.
A kiss of magic, bright and free,
Transcending time, just you and me.

They beckon us to join their play,
In meadows lush where children sway.
Under the boughs where dreams are spun,
With sunlit love, we greet the fun.

So lift your voice, let joy take wing,
As woodland fae to you will sing.
Embrace the light, let worries fade,
In sunbeams dancing, memories made.

A Tapestry Woven by Nature's Glow

In twilight's embrace, the world transforms,
With hues of gold, the heart conforms.
Each leaf a thread, each breeze a seam,
In nature's quilt, we find our dream.

The rivers whisper, stories untold,
Of mountains high and valleys bold.
With every stitch, the stars align,
A glimpse of magic, pure and divine.

Through meadows bright, the wildflowers dance,
In harmony, they weave romance.
A symphony of color and light,
Where every spirit takes to flight.

Beneath the moon, the shadows blend,
As night takes hold, whispers extend.
In every corner, wonder glows,
A tapestry woven by nature's throes.

So wander free through this gentle land,
Let beauty guide, take their hand.
In every moment, a treasure lies,
In nature's glow, the heart complies.

Saffron Shadows in Twilight's Embrace

As day surrenders to the night,
The saffron shadows bathe in light.
They stretch and dance, a fluid grace,
In twilight's hush, a warm embrace.

The fireflies twinkle, secrets shared,
In murmurs soft, our souls prepared.
Each heartbeat echoes, nature's song,
In woven whispers, we belong.

With every step, the air ignites,
As hues of orange paint the sights.
In gentle curls, the breezes sigh,
With stars awoken in velvet sky.

Hand in hand, we roam the vale,
Through saffron shadows, we shall sail.
With laughter light and hearts set free,
In twilight's glow, just you and me.

So gather close as darkness falls,
In tranquil woods, the night enthralls.
In whispers sweet, let dreams replace,
The worries of day in twilight's grace.

Shimmers of Enchantment in Hidden Landscapes

In valleys where the shadows play,
Soft whispers guide the night away.
A glimmer dances on the stream,
Where dreams entwine in a silver beam.

The bloom of stars in twilight's hold,
Unveils the wonders yet untold.
Each fluttering leaf seems to sigh,
As magic breathes beneath the sky.

Look close and find the hidden trails,
Where faeries weave their secret tales.
Beneath the boughs of ancient trees,
The breeze sings sweetly through the leaves.

A tapestry of twilight's grace,
Awakens joy in this sacred space.
With every step, the heart takes flight,
Into a realm where day meets night.

So wander forth with open heart,
Embrace the light, let shadows part.
For in each shimmer, life does share,
The beauty found in moments rare.

Golden Reflections in the Evening Mist

As daylight fades and secrets creep,
The world awakens from its sleep.
Golden hues wash over the glade,
As softest whispers serenade.

The river holds the sun's farewell,
In ripples where sweet stories dwell.
Each grain of sand, a memory spun,
While shadows dance beneath the sun.

The mist swirls gently, a veil so fine,
Weaving dreams with a magic line.
In twilight's glow, the heart feels free,
Caught in the web of mystery.

Upon the hill, a soft refrain,
Calls out to every heart's domain.
For hopes and wishes carried near,
Are wrapped in gold, free from fear.

So linger here while time stands still,
Awash in warmth, the evening chill.
Let golden echoes fill your mind,
As night unfolds, with wonders lined.

Ethereal Echoes through Whispering Pines

Through whispering pines where secrets dwell,
An echo sounds, a soothing spell.
Each breath of wind, a tale bestowed,
In nature's arms, where spirits strode.

The twilight calls, a tender sound,
As twilight skies embrace the ground.
With every rustle, stories grow,
In shadows deep, where dreams bestow.

The branches sway, a gentle dance,
Inviting souls to take a chance.
Among the roots, where life begins,
Ethereal echoes breathe like winds.

Each step reveals a hidden path,
Where laughter mingles with the past.
In every sigh of nature's breath,
Lies hope that deepens even death.

So heed the call of night's embrace,
As stars reflect on time and space.
For in these woods, so vast, serene,
Awaits the magic, evergreen.

The Luminous Heart of Enchanted Wanderings

In wanderings where starlight glows,
A luminous heart gently flows.
Each step unearthed in twilight's art,
Awakens treasures from the start.

With every breath, a new surprise,
As wonder dances in our eyes.
The nightingale's soft, tender song,
Guides weary hearts where they belong.

Through hidden paths, adventure waits,
Unlocking all the ancient gates.
For in the quiet, magic sleeps,
In every dream, a promise keeps.

The moonlight drapes the world in white,
As mysteries unfold in night.
With every pause, the heart will learn,
Of fires that in the darkness burn.

So follow where the whispers lead,
And listen close, let spirit heed.
For in enchanted wanderings bold,
Lies every story waiting to unfold.

The Veil of Dawn Among Faerie Blessings

In the hush of dawn's embrace,
Where whispers blend with light,
A veil of dreams in softest lace,
  The faeries take their flight.

They dance on dew-kissed blades so bright,
With laughter sweet and clear,
A symphony of pure delight,
That only hearts can hear.

Each bloom awakens with a sigh,
As petals stretch and yawn,
While vivid colors fill the sky,
In reverence to the dawn.

With gentle grace, the forest sways,
As secrets softly sway,
And in the light of morning's rays,
The faerie blessings play.

So linger here, in magic's thrall,
Where nature's wonders gleam,
For in this realm, we're free of all,
And caught within a dream.

Ethereal Pathways in Golden Moments

Through glades aglow with sunlight's grace,
An ethereal path unfolds,
Where every step, a soft embrace,
Of whispers and of gold.

The trees that arch like guardian sprites,
Bear witness to the dance,
While shadows twirl in playful flights,
Inviting hearts to chance.

In golden moments time stands still,
As laughter fills the air,
With every breath, a gentle thrill,
A promise everywhere.

Among the blooms that sway and spin,
The faeries weave their spell,
A tapestry where dreams begin,
In this enchanted dell.

So wander forth, with wonder wide,
And let your spirit soar,
For here in light and joy abide,
The glories to explore.

Enchanted Secrets of the Faerie Woodlands

In depths where whispers softly weave,
The faerie woodlands lie,
With secrets held that few believe,
Beneath the twilight sky.

The mossy paths that twist and twine,
Invite the brave to tread,
With every leaf, a tale divine,
Of magic, hopes, and dread.

A flicker here, a glint of light,
A shimmer in the air,
The secrets dance from night to night,
With faeries bold and fair.

In hidden nooks where shadows play,
And laughter floats like song,
The enchanted moments softly sway,
To where we all belong.

So pause and listen to the breeze,
The stories brought to you,
For in their whispers, hearts find ease,
And magic speaks anew.

The Light that Bends between Their Worlds

A light that bends between two realms,
In twilight's gentle grace,
Where faeries weave their lush diadems,
Of dreams in soft embrace.

The echoes of their laughter rise,
Like silver threads that weave,
Through shadows cast by starlit skies,
In places we believe.

With every flicker, visions dance,
Of journeys yet untold,
In whispered winds, they spin and prance,
Their magic to unfold.

The borders blur where hearts are free,
And wonder finds its way,
In moments lost in mystery,
Where night outshines the day.

So step between the worlds and see,
The light that beats within,
For in this realm, we are meant to be,
Where every spell begins.

A Tapestry of Glimmers Above Ferny Hollows

In the misty dawn, where shadows play,
Glimmers dance above, in soft ballet.
Whispers of secrets in the gentle breeze,
Ferny hollows cradle, with quiet ease.

The sunlight weaves through branches high,
Casting dreams where the lost ones lie.
A tapestry of light, stitched with care,
Nature's breath, a sigh of prayer.

Children of the forest, spirits so bright,
Chasing flickers of the fleeting light.
Underneath the canopy's tender sway,
They twirl and spin, in playful fray.

Each glimmer holds a story untold,
Of bravery, of love, and hearts bold.
In the ferny verdure, mysteries grow,
A world of wonders, forever aglow.

As twilight falls, with stars in sight,
The glow of faeries ignites the night.
Above the hollows, they weave their spell,
A symphony sung from their hidden well.

Radiant Kisses from the Faerie Realm

In the garden of dreams, where petals bloom,
Faeries flit softly, dispelling the gloom.
With radiant kisses upon every flower,
They breathe magic in the twilight hour.

Dewdrops glisten like jewels in the morn,
With each gentle touch, a new hope is born.
They gather the light of the rising sun,
Creating a dance, where all is one.

Every whisper carries a song of delight,
Echoing softly in the still of the night.
From the faerie realm, secrets unfold,
In colors and tales, both cherished and bold.

Around ancient trees, with roots deep and wide,
They play hide and seek, with joy as their guide.
Unseen yet felt, like a breeze on your cheek,
Their laughter and light, a magic unique.

When twilight descends, the faerie lights gleam,
Sending messages sweet, woven in dream.
In this enchanted realm, they linger near,
Radiant kisses, whispered with cheer.

Woodland Secrets in the Golden Luminance

In the heart of the woods, where shadows entwine,
Golden luminance glimmers, a sign divine.
Whispers of wisdom carried on the air,
Secrets of old, in the silence laid bare.

Beneath towering oaks, where the wildflowers sway,
Nature unfolds in a tranquil ballet.
Each petal and leaf tells a tale of grace,
Of woodland creatures, and their hidden place.

The sun bathes the forest in warming light,
Casting spells in the hush of the night.
A tapestry woven with threads of gold,
In the woodland's embrace, tales are retold.

Underneath the ferns, mysteries hide,
A labyrinth of wonders where shadows abide.
From dawn until dusk, in the charming glen,
Whispers of magic echo again and again.

As night draws near, and the stars appear,
The woodland awakens, curious and clear.
In golden luminance, secrets are shared,
A bond with the earth, forever declared.

The Hidden Glow of the Faerie Wood

In the depths of the grove, where few dare to tread,
The faerie wood whispers, with wonders widespread.
A hidden glow flickers like fireflies' flight,
Luring the hearts of those seeking light.

Veils of enchantment drape over each tree,
Cradling the laughter of souls wild and free.
Under moonlit skies, dreams take their shape,
In the heart of the wood, escapades escape.

Glimmers of laughter, and secrets to share,
With each step we take, we breathe in the air.
The warmth of the faeries, a comforting balm,
In the chaos of world, their presence is calm.

From blossoms to branches, the magic extends,
With whispers of kinship among ancient friends.
In the hidden glow, every heart can find,
A refuge of beauty, profound and kind.

So roam through the faerie wood, let time sway,
Lost in the shimmering night, where dreams play.
For within its embrace, we're never alone,
In the glow of the faerie wood, love is our home.

Beneath the Glimmering Canopy of Dreams

Beneath the canopy where whispers play,
The moonlight dances in a silver sway.
Stars sprinkle secrets on the mossy floor,
While dreams awaken from the darkened shore.

Gentle breezes hum a lullaby sweet,
As shadows glide on softly padded feet.
In this enchanted realm where fears dissolve,
The heart's desires begin to evolve.

Elfin laughter echoes through the night,
In every flicker, there's a spark of light.
Each sighing branch may tell a tale untold,
Of hopes and wishes woven into gold.

With every breath, new magic takes to flight,
As colors meld beneath the velvet night.
In dreams where wonder makes its bold advance,
We weave our lives in the grand, cosmic dance.

So linger here, where fantasies entwine,
And let the glimmer of this world be thine.
Through every moment, let your soul unfurl,
For beneath the canopy, awaits the world.

Mythic Journeys through Sun-dappled Realms

In sun-dappled realms where shadows play,
Mythic journeys beckon, come what may.
Through forests deep and skies so wide,
Adventure calls to hearts that yearn and bide.

With every step, a story starts to bloom,
Where ancient tales dispel the creeping gloom.
A treasure hidden in each rustling leaf,
Awaits the seeker who believes, not thief.

Through valleys lush and mountains proud and tall,
The whispers of the past in echoes call.
Guardians of wonder line the winding path,
Unraveling the magic in their wrath.

Beneath the arches of the towering trees,
The laughter of the forest rides the breeze.
Each moment breathes with possibilities,
In realms where dreams unfurl like golden leaves.

So take my hand and let the journey start,
As we exchange the mundane for the heart.
Through sun-dappled realms, our tales shall blend,
Mythic journeys await, around the bend.

The Elusive Glow of Woodland Mysteries

In the woodland's hush lies a soft glow,
Mysteries linger where few dare to go.
Every rustle holds a tale of old,
In the heart of the forest, secrets bold.

Gossamer threads weave a tapestry fine,
Guiding the curious toward the divine.
With every footfall, enchantment is spun,
As the shadows whisper of battles won.

Moonbeams caress the leaves in a dance,
While dreams awaken, slip into a trance.
Creatures of wonder peek from their lairs,
Inviting explorers to climb their stairs.

As dawn breaks gently, revealing the light,
The mysteries shimmer, taking to flight.
Each fleeting moment, a chance to behold,
The woodland's glow with adventures untold.

So wander the pathways where magic will seek,
In the foliage thick, let your spirit speak.
For the elk and the fox, and the owl too,
Guard the woodland's glow, waiting for you.

Dreams of Sapphire and Gold in Faerie Land

In faerie lands where skies in sapphire gleam,
And rivers flow like liquid gold in dream.
The flowers whisper secrets soft and low,
Of ancient magic only dreamers know.

A tapestry of starlight weaves the air,
With pixie laughter threading everywhere.
Each glimmering petal and sparkling dew,
Offers a taste of wonders ever new.

Beneath the willow, stories take their flight,
Bathed in the glow of the gentle night.
In dreams of color, where wishers can roam,
Faerie land beckons, whispering, "Come home."

With wings of shimmer, the fae dance and twirl,
Around the amber flames that softly swirl.
In each soft sigh, a promise is made,
In sapphire skies where dreams never fade.

So lose yourself in this magical thrall,
In faerie land, where enchantments enthrall.
With dreams of precious stones, bright and bold,
Take flight with wonders, let your heart unfold.

Sun-Kissed Secrets of the Woodland

In whispers soft, the trees confide,
A tale of magic, where secrets hide.
Beneath the leaves, in dappled light,
The woodland breathes, a wondrous sight.

With every step, the earth does sing,
Of hidden realms and ancient spring.
A sprite may dance, a fox may play,
In sun-kissed glades where shadows sway.

The brook will gurgle, the flowers bloom,
In nature's heart, there's no room for gloom.
A world alive, with colors bright,
Where dreams take flight in morning light.

Listen close to the rustling leaves,
For each one tells what nature weaves.
A story spun from bark and root,
In every corner, a secret suit.

In twilight hours, the glow unfolds,
With fireflies' light, the night beholds.
Sun-kissed secrets, forever kept,
In woodland's heart, where magic slept.

Adventures in the Amber-laced Wild

In amber glows, the wild unfurls,
Where sunlight dances and nature whirls.
With every step, adventure calls,
Where freedom sings and twilight falls.

A winding path through ferns and moss,
Each twist and turn a treasure's gloss.
A rustle here, a fleeting glance,
In amber dreams, we dare to dance.

Upon the hill, the skyline gleams,
With hues of gold and silver beams.
We'll climb the heights, through gales we'll soar,
In wild embrace, we'll seek for more.

Through bramble thick and thicket dense,
With whispers soft, we find our sense.
A hidden glen, a wildflower crown,
In amber dreams, our spirits drown.

And as the sun dips low and weak,
The wild takes on a mystic cheek.
In every shadow, adventures hide,
In amber-laced wild, our hearts abide.

Enigmatic Luminescence Amongst the Thickets

In thickets deep, where shadows play,
Enigmas swirl at close of day.
A lantern glow, a shimmering light,
In whispered dreams, they take their flight.

The moonlit paths, where echoes ring,
Hold stories of the night's soft wing.
With every rustle, secrets churn,
In luminous hues, we yearn and yearn.

With sighs of ancients in the air,
The thickets breathe a tale laid bare.
A dance of spirits, a flicker bright,
Enigmatic forms in velvet night.

Amongst the leaves, a glinting sheen,
Of mysteries veiled, both sly and keen.
We weave through stars, in twilight kissed,
As thickets sway, lost in a tryst.

And when the dawn breaks icy cold,
The secrets fade, but hearts are bold.
Amongst the thickets, we roam and seek,
In luminescence, our spirits speak.

Starlit Pathways to Dreamer's Enclave

Upon the starlit pathways wide,
Dreamer's enclave, our hearts abide.
With every step, the cosmos gleams,
In whispered hopes and silver dreams.

A melody of twinkling stars,
Leads softly to where magic spars.
Through twilight's veil, in silent grace,
We tread the line where time lays face.

In dreams unfurling, the night does weave,
A tapestry that we believe.
With every glance at skies above,
The universe wraps us in its love.

In hidden realms where moonbeams play,
We find ourselves, we drift, we sway.
The starlit pathways, a guide so true,
To dreamer's enclave, where wishes grew.

As dawn draws close, and night must flee,
The stars will fade, but we shall see.
In every heart, the dreams retain,
In starlit pathways, we'll meet again.